DISCOVER
Heredity

MW01113577

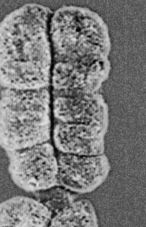

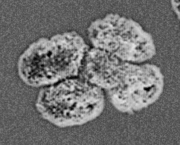

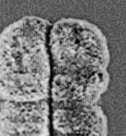

by Barbara Brannon

Table of Contents

Introduction

Some **traits** are because of **heredity**. Some traits are **talents**.

▲ We can look like our parents.

Words to Know

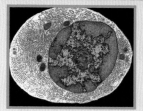

cells

chromosomes

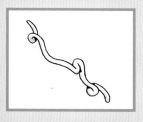

genes

heredity

talents

traits

▲ We can do things like our parents.

See the Glossary on page 22.

What Is Heredity?

Parents have **cells**.

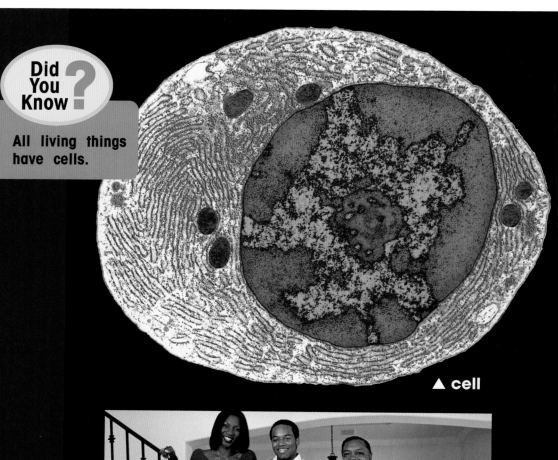

▲ cell

▲ People have millions of cells.

4

Cells have **chromosomes**.

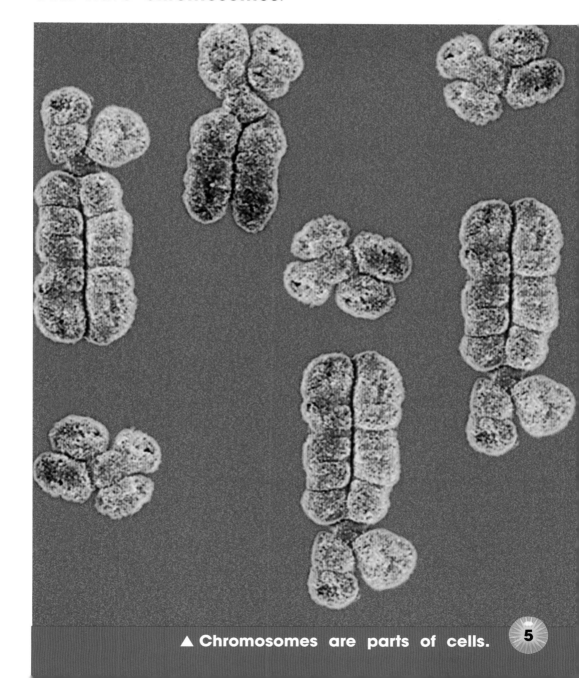

Chromosomes have **genes**.

cell

body

It's A Fact

You inherit genes from your parents. Your genes make you special.

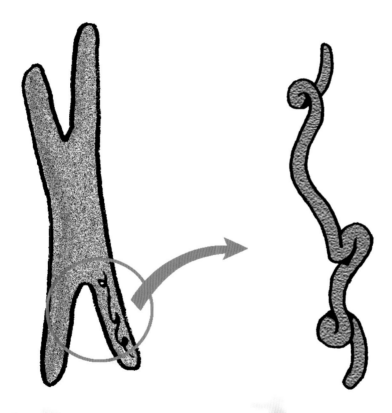

chromosome   gene

▲ Genes are on chromosomes.

What Traits Do We Inherit?

We inherit traits from our parents.

▲ **Children can look like their parents.**

We inherit body type.

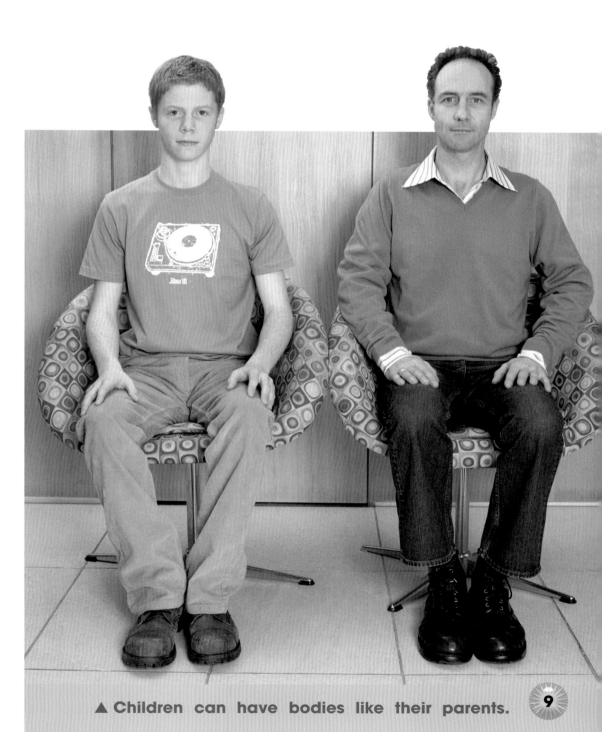

▲ **Children can have bodies like their parents.**

We inherit eye color.

Children can have eyes like their parents

We inherit skin color.

▲ Children can have skin like their parents.

We inherit hair color.

▲ Children can have hair like their parents.

We inherit height.

Which Traits Are Talents?

A parent can paint. Often the child can paint.

▲ Some children paint like their parents.

A parent can sing. Often the child can sing.

▲ Some children sing like their parents.

A parent can play baseball. Often the child can play baseball.

▲ Some children play baseball like their parents.

A parent can run fast. Often the child can run fast.

▲ Some children run like their parents.

A parent can play the piano. Often the child can play the piano.

▲ **Some children play the piano like their parents.**

Conclusion

We have cells. We have chromosomes. We have genes.

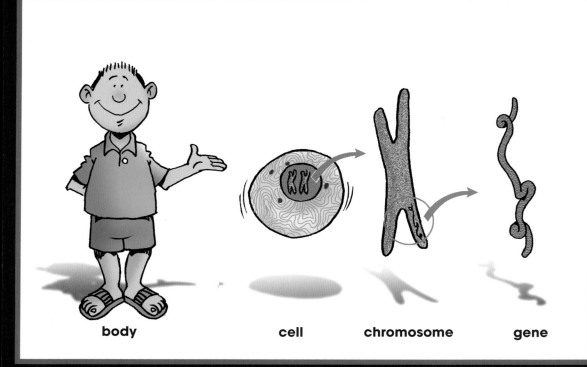

body   cell   chromosome   gene

We have different traits. We have different talents.

Concept Map

Heredity

What Is Heredity?

| cells |
| chromosomes |
| genes |

What Traits Do We Inherit?

| body type |
| eye color |
| skin color |
| hair color |
| height |

Which Traits Are Talents?

drawing
singing
playing baseball
running
playing piano

Glossary

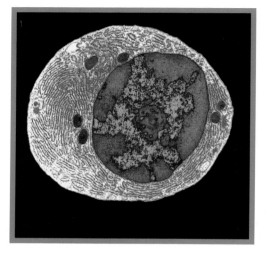

cells smallest parts of a living thing

*Parents have **cells**.*

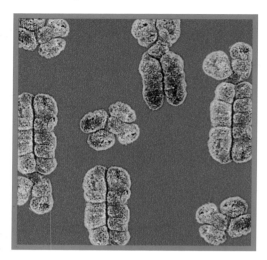

chromosomes parts of cells

*Cells have **chromosomes**.*

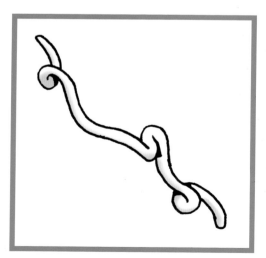

genes parts of chromosomes

*Chromosomes have **genes**.*

heredity parents passing on traits to children

*Some traits come from **heredity**.*

talents natural ability to do something well

*We have different **talents**.*

traits features of a person

*We inherit **traits** from our parents.*

Index